Parenting Through Mental Health Challenges
A Practical Guide

Developed by Glow For Hope NFP

Compiled and written by Kelly Poelker for Glow For Hope NFP

March 2026 Edition

This publication was developed by Glow For Hope NFP and compiled and written by Kelly Poelker.

Disclaimer

This guide is provided for educational and informational purposes only and does not constitute medical, psychological, or professional advice. Readers are encouraged to seek guidance from qualified healthcare providers.

This book incorporates research and information from various sources, which are cited throughout. The author claims fair use of copyrighted material under the guidelines of Section 107 of the U.S. Copyright Act for purposes of criticism, comment, scholarship, and research. All quoted or paraphrased material is attributed to its respective author and source.

ISBN: 978-0-9967202-3-6 (Print)

Published by: Glow For Hope Publishing (an imprint of Another 8 Hours Publishing)

Cover design by: Elizabeth Scott (enicholsdesign.com)

Edited by: Katy Balcer

glow FOR HOPE™

"A practical and accessible resource for parents, this guide offers thoughtful, evidence-informed support. We are excited to help share this meaningful tool with families in our community."

—St. Clair County Mental Health Board - Illinois

This whole book is amazing, but Part II offers valuable guidance to parents navigating difficult circumstances with their children. When Challenges Arise addresses complex mental health issues thoughtfully and provides clear, practical information that supports families without minimizing the challenges involved. The explanations are both compassionate and empowering, promoting a constructive approach to these concerns.

What I value most is the insight that noticing early signs isn't about putting a label on anyone; it's a way of showing genuine care for our children by stepping forward and finding help when it's needed. This section empowers parents to pause before acting, pay closer attention, answer with greater understanding, and act with bravery and compassion.

Thank you, Kelly, for caring so much.

Dr. Olivia Johnson, Author
The Tactical Pause for Teens

TABLE OF CONTENTS

A Letter from Our Founder

To Every Parent Who's Worried, Unsure, or Scared

Before you turn another page, take a breath...

We want to start by acknowledging something important:

You're here.

That alone speaks volumes.

You've come to this guide seeking answers, direction, and maybe even searching for hope. Perhaps you're tired. Perhaps you're scared. Perhaps you've already lived through some moments you never imagined you'd have to navigate with your child.

We see you.

Supporting a young person facing mental health challenges is one of the most courageous journeys you can walk. It is also one of the heaviest. And yet, here you are. Still showing up. Still asking the hard questions. Still holding space for healing, even when your own heart feels worn.

This guide was created for you—with deep empathy and respect.

It's not a textbook or a checklist. It wasn't written by a panel of distant, unseen professionals (though we've incorporated trusted, evidence-based research). Instead, this guide is rooted in lived experience and shaped by the voices of people who've walked this path—parents, caregivers, survivors, therapists, and advocates. It's filled with the knowledge we wish we'd had, the compassion we all need, and tools that can truly make a difference.

Here, you'll find:

- Practical, everyday strategies to support your child
- Gentle reminders that your well-being matters, too
- Encouragement to keep going, even when it's hard
- A sense of community—because you are not alone

We will talk about difficult things. We'll also touch on resilience, small victories, and the power of unconditional love. Most of all, we'll remind you that no one expects perfection. What matters is presence. Connection. Compassion.

So, wherever you are on this journey, know this:

You are doing better than you think.

Your presence here is an act of love.

This guide is our offering to walk beside you with understanding, guidance, and hope.

With love and light,

Kelly Poelker

Kelly Poelker
Founder, Glow For Hope

How to Use This Guide

This guide is designed to meet you where you are.

You do **not** need to read it cover to cover in one sitting. Parenting through mental health challenges is not linear — and neither is this book. You may find yourself returning to certain sections, skipping others for now, or moving back and forth depending on what your family needs at any given moment.

Here's how the guide is structured:

- **Part I** lays the foundation. It focuses on understanding youth mental health, building emotional safety, and strengthening connections.
- **Part II** helps you recognize challenges as they form and deepen, and introduces common mental health conditions and risk factors.
- **Part III** offers practical parenting tools and communication strategies that can be used in many everyday moments.
- **Parts IV–VI** address special considerations, caregiver support, and moving forward with hope.

Throughout the guide, you'll see reminders such as *"we'll explore this more later"* or *"see another section for deeper support."* These are intentional. You are not expected to master everything at once.

Use this guide as a reference, a companion, and a reassurance that you don't have to tackle this all on your own. Take what helps. Set down what feels like too much. You can always come back.

Part I: Understanding Youth Mental Health

Introduction: Why Mental Health Matters

Let's begin by understanding why mental health matters, and why supporting it early, consistently, and compassionately makes such a profound difference in our children's lives.

Firstly, it's crucial to recognize that mental health issues are as real and significant as physical health problems. Just as you wouldn't dismiss a broken leg or high fever, mental health conditions deserve the same level of attention and care. Unfortunately, some older generations may view mental health struggles as more controllable or even imaginary. Acknowledging the legitimacy of these issues is a vital step toward providing effective support.

When discussing your child's mental health, it's important to approach the conversation with empathy and understanding. Avoid overwhelming them with a barrage of questions, which can cause them to shut down. Instead, create a safe and open space for them to share their feelings at their own pace. Studies have shown that empathetic communication can impact a child's mental health outcomes significantly.

Try to resist the urge to highlight all the good things in their life or to suggest they should "count their blessings." While well-intentioned,

Mental Health vs. Physical Health:

The idea that mental health issues are as significant as physical health issues is supported by research. The World Health Organization (WHO) has consistently advocated for treating mental health with the same urgency as physical health, emphasizing that mental health conditions can be just as debilitating as chronic physical conditions.[1]

[1] World Health Organization. "Mental Health: Strengthening O Response." 2020. WHO.

these comments can minimize a child's feelings and make them feel misunderstood.[2] It's more beneficial to validate their emotions and experiences, letting them know that it's okay to feel the way they do.

We can't stress this point enough–validation of feelings. You may think what upset your child at school today is the silliest little thing. But to them, it's huge. Put yourself in their shoes. Think back to a time when you shared with someone, maybe your spouse or significant other, about something that happened at work which had you really upset. How did it feel to you when their reaction was, "I don't know why you're making such a big deal out of it. It was nothing; just move on." You likely felt completely dismissed, like your feelings didn't matter.

Or how about a time when you were young and complained to your parents about not having something that everyone else had. What if their reaction to your expression was, "People in other countries have it so much worse. You ought to feel lucky to have what you do." It's the same with your own child. Feelings are real to the person feeling them. We don't have to agree with them completely, though we do need to acknowledge that we're sorry they are feeling badly. Or that you can see how frustrating it can be to experience disappointment or strife.

Navigating these conversations requires a delicate balance. Parents need to distinguish between genuine distress and potential manipulation[3] while maintaining their composure and setting clear boundaries. By listening actively, validating emotions, and seeking out professional help when necessary, parents can support their child's mental well-being effectively.

---

[2] *The advice against minimizing a child's feelings by emphasizing positive aspects of their life is rooted in cognitive-behavioral therapy (CBT) principles, where validation of emotions is crucial for therapeutic progress.* **Reference:** Linehan, M. M. (1993). "Cognitive-Behavioral Treatment of Borderline Personality Disorder." Guilford Press.

[3] *We use the term manipulation with caution, as it can be viewed as a stigmatizing word on the receiving end. Often what parents see as manipulation is actually the youth trying to get some sort of need met, albeit in a negative manner.*

Remember, you are not alone in this journey.

Together, we can create a supportive environment where our children feel safe, understood, and cared for—building a strong foundation that supports mental well-being and reduces risk over time.

Tips for Nurturing Your Child's Mental Wellness

A Note for Parents: The strategies below are meant to offer guidance — not a checklist. You are not expected to implement everything at once. Consider this section a menu of supportive practices you can return to as your child grows and circumstances change.

Building Connection & Emotional Safety

Nurturing your child's mental wellness is not about having all the right answers, it's about creating a safe, supportive, and compassionate space where your child feels seen, heard, and valued. Mental health is a journey, not a destination, and it evolves with your child's age, experiences, and environment. In this section, you'll find practical tips rooted in empathy, connection, and everyday actions. Whether you're responding to early signs of emotional distress or looking for ways to proactively support your child's well-being, these insights are designed to guide and encourage you. Remember: the most powerful thing you can offer your child is your presence and your willingness to walk alongside them—one step at a time.

Educate yourself about your child's specific mental health condition

Take the time to research and understand your child's diagnosis.[4] Learn about the symptoms, treatment options, and potential challenges associated with their condition. Knowledge is empowering and will help you advocate for your child's needs effectively.

(More on Mental Health Disorders - See page 27)

Foster open and honest communication with your child

Again, you want to create an environment where your child feels comfortable expressing their thoughts and feelings. Encourage regular conversations about how they're feeling and what they're experiencing. Listen attentively and without judgment, validating their emotions and experiences.

Create a safe and supportive home environment

Establish a home environment that promotes emotional safety and security. Provide love, acceptance, and encouragement to your child, while repeatedly emphasizing that your home is a place where they can be themselves without fear of judgment or criticism. But it's more than words. The real work is in making it so—in the daily choices, reactions, and moments that will either build that safety or quietly chip away at it. Your child will feel the difference between a home that talks about acceptance and one that truly gives it.

Encourage your child to express their feelings without judgment

Help your child develop healthy coping mechanisms for expressing their emotions. Teach them that it's okay to feel sad, angry, or anxious and provide them with constructive outlets for expressing their feelings.

Visit the Glow For Hope Resource Hub for more support, tools, and downloadable resources.

[4] *Studies show that informed parents can better advocate for their child's needs.*
Reference: National Institute of Mental Health (NIMH). "Parents and Caregivers." NIMH

Seek support from mental health professionals and support groups

Don't hesitate to reach out for professional help when needed. Mental health professionals[5] can provide invaluable support and guidance for both you and your child. Additionally, consider joining a support group for families with similar health conditions to connect with others who understand what you're going through.

Take care of yourself—you matter too

This is one of the most important things to remember, so please do not skip over this one! When you're in the thick of supporting a child through mental health challenges, your own needs can feel selfish to even think about. They're not. You cannot show up consistently for your child if you're running on empty, and guilt won't fill that tank back up. Take the break. Ask for help. Forgive yourself for the moments you didn't handle perfectly. Be as patient with your own progress as you're trying to be with theirs. None of this makes you a less devoted parent. It makes you a sustainable one.

Be your child's strongest advocate

Work collaboratively with your child's school to ensure your child receives the support they need to succeed academically and socially. Advocate for accommodations[6], such as extra time on tests or access to counseling services, and stay informed about your child's progress and challenges at school. When it comes to advocating for your child, the school is just the beginning.

---

[5]*Engaging with mental health professionals and peer support groups is a cornerstone of effective mental health care, validated by numerous studies that show improved outcomes through professional intervention and community support.* **Reference:** Peer Support Research. (2020). Mental Health America link.

[6]*IDEA (Individuals with Disabilities Education Act) and Section 504 plans are frameworks for advocating for these needs.*

You are your child's most important advocate, and that role matters more than you might realize. Insurance denials, long waitlists, school systems that move slowly, providers who don't quite fit. These are real obstacles and navigating them will take persistence. Don't be afraid to make the calls, ask the hard questions, request second opinions, or push back when something doesn't feel right. You know your child better than any system does. That knowledge is your most powerful tool, and using it on their behalf is one of the most concrete ways that love shows up in this journey.

Establish consistent routines to provide structure and stability

Consistent routines can help your child feel more secure and in control. When so much of life feels unpredictable or overwhelming, knowing what comes next—a regular mealtime, a familiar bedtime routine, a designated wind-down period—gives the nervous system something steady to hold on to. You don't need an overly rigid schedule, and some days it simply won't go as planned. But returning to the same rhythms as often as you can will send a powerful message to your child: this home is a safe and predictable place, and you are taken care of here.

Encourage healthy habits, including regular exercise and balanced nutrition

Physical health and mental health are far more connected than most people realize. Regular movement—even a daily walk, a bike ride, or shooting hoops in the driveway—can meaningfully reduce anxiety and improve mood. Nutritious meals matter too, not as a performance of perfect parenting, but because what we put in our bodies genuinely affects how we feel. You don't have to overhaul everything at once. Start with small, sustainable habits and build from there. Modeling these habits yourself goes a long way, too.

Monitor your child's social media and screen time usage

Be mindful of the impact of screen time and social media on your child's mental health. Monitor their online activities and set limits on screen time to ensure they have plenty of time and energy for other activities that promote social interaction and relaxation, as recommended by the American Academy of Pediatrics.[7]

Social media isn't inherently harmful, though research increasingly links heavy use in adolescents to higher rates of anxiety, depression, loneliness, and poor sleep. The goal isn't to eliminate it. It's to stay curious about how it's making your child feel.

Teach your child coping strategies for managing stress and anxiety

Help your child develop healthy coping mechanisms for managing stress and anxiety. Teach them relaxation techniques, like deep breathing, progressive muscle relaxation, or mindfulness. Encourage them to practice these techniques regularly to build resilience and find calm in moments of distress. Providing your child with these tools can empower them to manage their emotions more effectively and reduce overall stress levels.[8]

Visit the Glow For Hope Resource Hub for more support

[7]American Academy of Pediatrics, Council on Communications and Media. (2016). *Media use in school-aged children and adolescents. Pediatrics,* 138(5), e20162592. https://doi.org/10.1542/peds.2016-2592

[8]*Beck, A. T. (2011). Cognitive Behavior Therapy: Basics and Beyond. Guilford Press.*

Watch for these signs that social media may be affecting their mental health:

- increased irritabilit
- sadness after time on their phone,
- negative self-comparison to others they follow,
- anxiety when they can't access their device, or
- lost sleep to stay online late at night

A few things that can help:

- keep devices out o bedrooms at night,
- ask how social media makes them feel rather than jus monitoring,
- how much time they spend, and
- model the phone habits you want to see.

Set realistic expectations for your child's academic and extracurricular activities

Be realistic about what your child can handle, given their mental health challenges. Set achievable goals and prioritize their well-being over academic or extracurricular achievements.[9] This can be a little tricky, especially if your child was a high achiever before their struggles began or if you're feeling pressure from schools, coaches, or extended family.

It helps to reframe what success looks like during this season. Showing up on a hard day is a win. Finishing one assignment when everything feels impossible is a win. Progress during mental health challenges rarely looks like the progress we're used to measuring, and adjusting that measuring stick isn't lowering the bar. It's meeting your child where they are.

Be patient, understanding, and supportive during periods of emotional distress

Understand that your child may experience periods of emotional distress or instability. Be patient and supportive, offering comfort and reassurance without minimizing their feelings or experiences. During difficult times, provide a steady presence and remind them that you're there to help them through whatever challenges they're facing. It's essential to remain calm and composed, even when you feel overwhelmed, as your stability can offer a sense of security and support for your child.

Celebrate your child's achievements, no matter how small

Acknowledge their efforts and progress, boosting their self-esteem and motivation. Whether it's completing a therapy session or reaching a personal goal, acknowledge their achievements and offer encouragement. Take the time to praise your child regularly, not just point out the things

[9] *Setting realistic expectations helps prevent undue stress on children, especially those with mental health conditions. Research supports goal setting that aligns with a child's capabilities.* **Reference:** Locke, E. A., & Latham, G. P. (2002). Building a practically useful theory of goal setting and task motivation. *American Psychologist*, 57(9), 705-717.

they do wrong. This can make all the difference in the world for helping them develop a sense of self-worth instead of growing up feeling like they can't get anything right.

Practice active listening when your child wants to talk

Give them your full attention, maintain eye contact, and avoid interrupting or judging. Reflect back what you hear to ensure you understand their perspective.

Validate your child's emotions and experiences, no matter what

Let your child know their feelings are real and worthy of acknowledgment, even when you don't fully understand them or agree with them. Avoid the urge to minimize or fix—sometimes the most powerful thing you can offer is simply saying "I hear you, and I'm sorry you're feeling that way." When children feel genuinely seen, they're far more likely to keep talking, keep trusting, and to reach out for help when they really need it.

Lean on your faith for comfort

Turn to your faith for strength and guidance during challenging times. This looks different for everyone, and there's no single right way to do it. For some families it means prayer, for others it's community, ritual, or simply the quiet comfort of believing that something larger is holding you. Whatever form it takes for you, don't underestimate it as a source of resilience. And if your child is old enough, inviting them into that practice, even in small ways, can give them something steady to hold on to when everything else feels uncertain.

Involve your child in decision-making about their treatment plan

Empower your child to take an active role in their own care, respecting their

[10]*Involving patients in their treatment decisions is part of patient-centered care, which improves treatment adherence and outcomes.* **Reference:** Barry, M. J., & Edgman-Levitan, S. (2012). Shared decision making—pinnacle of patient-centered care. *New England Journal of Medicine*, 366(9), 780-781.

preferences and autonomy.[10] This is especially important for older children and teens, who are more likely to engage when they feel heard and included.

Even younger children benefit from being part of the process. While they may not fully understand everything, creating a sense of involvement can build trust and positively influence their willingness to participate.

Foster connections with supportive friends and family members

It can be tempting to pull inward when things get hard. You may find that you do this without even noticing it as a way to protect your child's privacy, avoid difficult questions, or if you simply do not have the energy to explain what's going on. But isolation tends to make everything heavier. Even one or two people who genuinely show up—a sibling, a neighbor, an old friend—can make a real difference for both you and your child. You don't have to share everything. The key is to let someone in.

Model healthy behaviors and coping mechanisms for your child

Be a positive role model for your child by demonstrating healthy behaviors and coping mechanisms. Show them your ways to manage stress, communicate effectively, and prioritize self-care. ***(Visit the Glow For Hope Resource Hub for more support).***

Your child is watching you more than you realize. When they see you take a breath before responding to something frustrating, talk openly about your own hard days, or ask for help when you need it, they learn that those reactions are okay—and possible. You don't have to be perfect. In fact, letting your child see you try, struggle, and keep going anyway are powerful lessons you can teach them. We tend to think showing vulnerability makes us weak in the eyes of our children. That simply is not true.

Looking Ahead: This topic is explored in greater depth in **Part II** and **Part III**, where we discuss warning signs, safety planning, and how to respond with calm and care.

Monitor for signs of self-harm or suicidal ideation

Look for warning signs such as changes in behavior, expressions of hopelessness, or talk about death or suicide. If you're concerned, seek help immediately. In an emergency, dial 911. If there is no immediate danger, start with your child's pediatrician (if you don't currently have a suitable mental health professional to consult), or reach out via phone (or text "HOPE") to dial 988, the Suicide and Crisis Lifeline.

Create a crisis plan in case of emergencies

Develop a crisis plan in collaboration with your child's mental health care team. Include emergency contact numbers, coping strategies, and steps to take in the event of a mental health crisis.

Visit the Glow For Hope Resource Hub for Safety Plan downloads.

Encourage your child to keep a journal to express their thoughts and feelings

Writing in a journal can be a powerful tool for emotional release and self-reflection. Research suggests that expressive writing helps individuals process difficult emotions, reduces stress, and can lead to greater mental clarity and emotional healing.[11] Journaling helps children understand their feelings and gain insight into their experiences, promoting self-awareness and emotional regulation.

Avoid blaming or shaming your child for their mental health struggles

Instead, offer empathy, understanding, and unconditional support. Blame and shame can exacerbate mental health issues, leading to feelings of guilt and low self-esteem. A supportive, non-judgmental approach fosters trust and encourages open communication. Studies show that families who offer empathy and validation instead of blame tend to create more positive environments for recovery and emotional growth.[12]

[11] Pennebaker, 1997
[12] Rogers, 1957

Advocate for greater awareness and understanding of mental health issues in your community

Stigma surrounding mental health is a significant barrier to seeking help. By advocating for awareness and educating others, families can help reduce stigma and create more inclusive environments for mental health support. Community engagement plays a key role in promoting understanding and reducing discrimination.[13] This advocacy can help improve access to resources and foster a more supportive network for those facing mental health challenges.

Learn how to get involved with Glow For Hope and support mental health awareness in your community.

Be flexible and adaptable in your approach to parenting

No two children are the same—and honestly, no two *days* are the same when you're parenting through mental health challenges. What worked last Tuesday may not work today, and that's not a failure on your part. It's just the nature of this journey. Give yourself permission to adjust, try something different, and trust that staying responsive to your child's changing needs matters far more than sticking to any single approach.

Encourage your child to engage in volunteer work or community service

Helping others can provide a sense of purpose and fulfillment, boosting your child's mood and self-esteem. Volunteer work has been linked to higher levels of happiness and mental well-being, especially for young people.[14]

Monitor for signs of substance abuse or other risky behaviors

In all honesty... By the time a parent notices something, their child has

[13]Corrigan et al., 2014
[14]Thoits & Hewitt, 2001

usually been struggling for a while. That's not a criticism; it's just how it tends to go. So, if something feels off, trust that instinct. Your gut is usually right on point. Changes in behavior, new secrecy, shifting friend groups, or a sudden drop in how much they care about things they used to love can all be worth a conversation. You don't need proof before you check in. Concern is enough of a reason.

Create a support network of other parents facing similar challenges

There is something uniquely comforting about talking to someone who truly gets it. Not because they read about it, but because they've lived it. Seek out other parents navigating similar challenges, whether through a local support group, an online community, or even one trusted friend in a similar situation. You don't have to have answers for each other. Sometimes just knowing you're not the only one is enough.

Connecting with others who understand your experience can provide validation, empathy, and practical advice that even the best professionals can't always offer. It can also remind you that you are not failing, you are simply navigating something genuinely difficult, alongside people who know exactly what that feels like. *(For more on building your support network, see Part V: Support for Parents.)*

Encourage your child to express themselves and their creativity through art, music, or writing

Sometimes the feelings that are hardest to say out loud can find their way out into the world through color from a paintbrush, notes from a guitar, or writing on a page. Creative expression gives children and teens a private, pressure-free method to process what they're going through, without having to find "the right words" or worry about anyone else's reaction. It doesn't matter whether they're talented. That's not the point. A sketchbook left on the kitchen table, a playlist they're allowed to lose themselves in, a journal with no rules about what goes inside. Each of these small invitations can open doors that direct conversation sometimes can't.

If your child resists the idea of "being creative," don't push the label. Ask what they enjoy. Ask what makes time feel like it disappears. That's usually where the outlet already lives. Your job is to try to notice it and give them more room to go there.

Visit the Glow For Hope Resource Hub for curated tools and resources to support your child's creative journey, including music playlists designed with mental wellness in mind.

Seek opportunities for your child to build self-esteem and confidence

Every child has something they're good at, even if it takes some searching to find it. Your job isn't to manufacture confidence through praise alone, but to help them discover what makes them feel capable. That might be sports, animals, cooking, building things, or helping younger kids. When a child finds an activity they can point to and say, "I'm good at this," it changes how they see themselves. Pay attention to what lights them up. Then find ways to give them more of it.

Encourage your child to set goals and work toward them at their own pace

When life feels heavy, it can be hard to see past today. Through thinking out loud, you and a child struggling with their mental health can build bridges to their future—not with pressure or big expectations, but with small, hopeful questions, like, *What do you want to try someday? What's something you're looking forward to? What does a good day look like for you?*

Research shows that the brain is naturally future-oriented, and that people with depression often struggle to imagine positive things ahead. Helping your child practice forward thinking—even in small doses—can gently reactivate that part of how their mind works. Goals don't have to be big. A plan to watch a new movie next weekend, try a new recipe, or reach out to a friend counts. What matters is helping them pinpoint something to move toward, one small step at a time.

Be patient with yourself and your child's progress

Recovery from mental health challenges takes time. Patience and understanding are essential to supporting your child's long-term well-being.

In some cases, mental health challenges may be ongoing, though with early awareness and the right support, they can be managed in a way that allows your child to grow and adapt.

Educating both yourself and your child about their experiences can make a meaningful difference. The earlier you begin to understand how to cope and manage these challenges, the more confident and prepared you will feel navigating the journey together.

Remind your child that they are not defined by their mental health condition

Tell your child that a diagnosis does not define who they are. It is just one part of their experience, not their whole identity.

Encourage them to recognize their strengths, interests, and the qualities that make them who they are beyond any challenges they may be facing. When children begin to see themselves only through the lens of a diagnosis, it can limit their confidence and sense of possibility. Helping them maintain a broader view of themselves supports resilience and self-worth.

This perspective has been echoed in conversations on the *Glow For Hope: Sparking Conversation on Mental Health Podcast*, where guests have emphasized the importance of separating a person's identity from their mental health struggles. When we help those living with mental health disorders understand they are more than what they're going through, we give them space to move forward, with hope and a deeper understanding of their diagnosis.

Encourage healthy boundaries with friends and family members

Teach your child to prioritize their own needs and well-being, even if it means saying no to others. Role-play scenarios to practice saying no respectfully and standing firm on decisions without apologizing excessively. When situations arise in which it seems like the child is simply not wanting to do what they're told, as a parent or trusted adult, handle it by having open, respectful conversations about their feelings and reasons for their decisions. Emphasize mutual respect and understanding while reinforcing the value of healthy boundaries. Help them understand that setting boundaries is a sign of strength and self-respect, not weakness, by encouraging assertive communication through which they express their needs confidently and clearly.

Stay hopeful and optimistic about your child's future

Maintaining hope and optimism is crucial for both parents and children. Hope has been shown to significantly influence positive mental health outcomes, resilience, and motivation in overcoming challenges. Research suggests that a parent's hopeful outlook is genuinely contagious; children who see their caregivers approach difficulty with steady optimism are more likely to internalize that same positive belief over time. You don't need all the answers; you simply need to keep showing them that a path forward exists. *(See Part VI: Moving Forward in Hope.)*

Practice gratitude and focus on the positive aspects of your child's life

This one comes with an important distinction. Gratitude is not about pretending things are fine when they aren't, and it's not about minimizing what your child is going through. Earlier we talked about how telling a child to "count their blessings" can make them feel dismissed, and the same applies to how we talk to ourselves as parents.

What gratitude actually looks like in this context is more subtle than that. It could be pausing to notice the moment your child laughed at something today. It's recognizing that they made it through a hard week. It's appreciating the small signs of progress that are easy to overlook when you're only focused on what's still broken. These moments don't cancel out the hard ones. But training yourself to notice them—really notice them—can keep you from losing sight of the bigger picture when things feel overwhelming. As a result, when your child sees you genuinely celebrating small victories rather than waiting for big ones, they'll begin to learn that their progress matters, exactly as it is.

Encourage your child to develop a support system of trusted friends and mentors

Your relationship with your child is irreplaceable, but it was never meant to be their only source of support. Kids and teens often open up differently to a coach, an aunt, a friend's parent, or a mentor than they do at home, and that's not a reflection on you. So don't take it personally. It's just how people work. Encourage those connections. Take note of who your child seems to trust and feel good around, and find small ways to nurture those relationships. A child who can count on even one trusted adult outside the home now has a meaningful safety net that extends well beyond what any single parent can provide.

It's also important to respect that relationship. If your child is opening up to someone outside the home, resist the urge to go back to that person expecting a full report of every conversation. The value of that connection lies precisely in the fact that your child feels safe there—safe enough to say things they may not be ready to say to you yet. That trust is sacred. Protecting it, even when your parental self wants every detail, is how you show your child their healing matters more than your own peace of mind.

Help your child understand that mental health conditions are not their fault

Mental health conditions don't develop because of weakness, bad choices, or poor parenting. They arise from a complex mix of factors—biology, genetics, life experiences, and environment—often in ways that are entirely outside anyone's control. Helping your child understand this isn't about making excuses. It's about freeing them from the weight of shame so that they can focus their energy on healing rather than self-blame. A child who believes their condition is a moral failing will struggle far more than one who understands it as something that happened to them, not something they caused.

Assist with scheduling doctor or therapy appointments and managing prescription medication orders and refills. When a child is struggling, the logistics of their own care can feel completely overwhelming, or even impossible to initiate on their own. Stepping in to handle these details is love in action, and exactly what being there looks like.

Part II: When Challenges Arise

Recognizing the Signs of Struggle

Even with the best prevention efforts, challenges can still arise. This section will help you recognize when your child may be struggling, and what to do next.

The following pages highlight some of the most common mental health conditions in youth, along with behaviors you may notice at home or school. This information isn't meant for self-diagnosis or labeling. Instead, it's a guide to help you understand what you're seeing and identify when it may be time to seek professional support or further evaluation.

1. Depression (Major Depressive Disorder)

- **Description:** Depression is a mood disorder characterized by persistent sadness, hopelessness, loss of interest in activities, and feelings of worthlessness or guilt.
- **Contribution:** Depression significantly lowers a person's ability to see hope for the future. It distorts thoughts, making individuals feel like their pain is permanent and unchangeable, which can drive suicidal ideation as a perceived "solution" to end suffering.

Children and teens with depression often feel like their pain is permanent or that things will never get better. These thoughts can cloud judgment and lead to isolation. Compassionate listening, daily structure, and professional help can make an enormous difference.

2. Bipolar Disorder

- **Description:** Bipolar disorder involves extreme mood swings between manic (high-energy, impulsive) and depressive (low-energy, hopeless) episodes.
- **Contribution:** During depressive episodes, individuals experience similar risks as with major depression. During manic episodes, impulsivity can

lead to unplanned suicidal behaviors. The unpredictability of these shifts can exacerbate hopelessness and risk.

During depressive periods, young people may feel heavy and unmotivated, while during manic periods they may act impulsively or take risks. These shifting emotions can be confusing and scary for both child and parent, but understanding the pattern helps families respond with patience and consistency.

3. Post-Traumatic Stress Disorder (PTSD)

- **Description:** PTSD develops after experiencing or witnessing traumatic events. It includes symptoms like flashbacks, nightmares, hypervigilance, and emotional numbness.
- **Contribution:** Intrusive memories, intense emotional pain, and feelings of being "stuck" in trauma can lead to despair and suicidal thoughts as a way to escape overwhelming distress.

Young people may appear distant or hypervigilant, often trying to avoid situations that remind them of what happened. Gentle reassurance, therapy, and a predictable environment can help them begin to feel safe again.

4. Schizophrenia and Other Psychotic Disorders

- **Description:** Schizophrenia is characterized by delusions, hallucinations, disorganized thinking, and impaired reality perception.
- **Contribution:** Psychotic symptoms like commanding auditory hallucinations ("voices") telling individuals to harm themselves, along with feelings of isolation or paranoia, can directly trigger suicidal actions.

Teens may describe hearing voices or seeing things others don't. This can be frightening and isolating. With early treatment, structure, and family support, many individuals can manage symptoms and live meaningful lives.

5. Borderline Personality Disorder (BPD)

- **Description:** BPD involves emotional instability, fear of abandonment, impulsive behaviors, and a pattern of intense and unstable relationships.
- **Contribution:** Individuals with BPD often experience chronic feelings of emptiness and intense emotional pain. Suicidal thoughts may be impulsive responses to overwhelming emotions, relationship turmoil, or perceived rejection.

Teens or young adults may experience deep sadness one moment and anger the next or feel empty and unsure of who they are. Consistent reassurance, boundaries, and access to therapy focused on emotional regulation can greatly improve stability and well-being.

6. Anxiety Disorders (Generalized Anxiety, Panic Disorder)

- **Description:** Anxiety disorders involve excessive worry, fear, or panic that interferes with daily life.
- **Contribution:** Severe, persistent anxiety can lead to exhaustion and feelings of being overwhelmed. The inability to manage this emotional distress may contribute to suicidal thoughts as a means of escape.

Children may seem restless, avoid certain activities, or complain of headaches and stomach aches. Chronic anxiety can be exhausting but teaching coping skills like deep breathing and grounding, and offering continued reassurance that they are safe, can provide real relief.

7. Substance Use Disorders

- **Description:** Substance use disorder involves compulsive use of alcohol or drugs despite negative consequences.
- **Contribution:** Substance abuse can exacerbate existing mental health issues and impair judgment. It often serves as an escape from pain, but increases impulsivity, which can lead to suicidal actions, especially during intoxication or withdrawal.

Youth may turn to substances to cope with emotional pain or social pressure. Substance use can worsen underlying mental health challenges and increase impulsivity. Addressing both substance use and emotional well-being together—without shame—creates a path toward recovery.

8. Eating Disorders (e.g. Anorexia Nervosa, Bulimia Nervosa)

- **Description:** Eating disorders involve extreme behaviors, thoughts, and emotions around food, weight, and body image.
- **Contribution:** The physical and emotional toll of eating disorders—like malnutrition, shame, and isolation—can contribute to despair and suicidal thoughts. Anorexia nervosa has one of the highest mortality rates among mental health conditions.

Teens may restrict eating, purge, or over-exercise, often stemming from deep emotional pain or perfectionism. These disorders can be life-threatening and require professional support, but recovery is possible when families respond with empathy and a focus on healing, not appearance.

9. Obsessive-Compulsive Disorder (OCD)

- **Description:** OCD is characterized by intrusive, distressing thoughts (obsessions) and repetitive behaviors (compulsions) aimed at reducing anxiety.
- **Contribution:** The relentless cycle of obsessions and compulsions can become overwhelming, leading individuals to feel trapped. This chronic stress and frustration can increase suicidal risk.

Children may feel trapped in cycles of rituals—like constant checking or cleaning—and become distressed when they can't complete them. Recognizing these behaviors as anxiety-driven, not defiance, helps parents respond with understanding and seek proper care.

10. Adjustment Disorders

- **Description:** Adjustment disorders occur when someone has difficulty coping with significant life changes or stressors.
- **Contribution:** Acute stress and feelings of helplessness can cause suicidal thoughts, particularly when individuals feel unable to adapt or recover from life changes.

Symptoms may include sadness, anxiety, or irritability. While often temporary, these feelings are very real to the child. Providing time, reassurance, and consistent routines helps them regain a sense of stability.

11. Attention-Deficit/Hyperactivity Disorder (ADHD)

- **Description:** ADHD is a neurodevelopmental disorder characterized by persistent patterns of inattention, hyperactivity, and impulsivity that interfere with functioning or development. Children and teens with ADHD may struggle with focus, following instructions, organization, or sitting still. Symptoms can look different depending on whether the presentation is primarily inattentive, hyperactive/impulsive, or combined.
- **Contribution:** Untreated ADHD can lead to academic difficulties, low self-esteem, frustration, and frequent conflict with parents, teachers, and peers. These struggles can contribute to feelings of failure, rejection, and isolation. Because ADHD often coexists with anxiety or depression, the emotional toll can increase the risk of suicidal ideation if the child begins to feel "broken" or "bad." Early recognition, structure, and compassionate support significantly reduce risk and improve outcomes.

Children with ADHD may struggle to sit still, pay attention, or complete tasks without becoming distracted. These behaviors can lead to frustration, self-blame, or conflict with adults who misunderstand them. Early recognition, supportive routines, and consistent communication help children feel capable and understood.

12. Oppositional Defiant Disorder (ODD)

- **Description:** ODD is a behavioral disorder marked by ongoing patterns of angry or irritable mood, argumentative or defiant behavior, and vindictiveness toward authority figures lasting at least six months. Children with ODD are not simply "rebellious"—their behavior often stems from emotional dysregulation, frustration intolerance, or underlying anxiety, depression, or trauma.
- **Contribution:** Without understanding and proper support, ODD can cause significant family conflict, strained relationships, and academic challenges. These children may internalize guilt or shame when punished for behaviors they cannot yet regulate. Misinterpreting ODD as intentional defiance rather than emotional struggle can escalate tension and increase mental health risks. Parental empathy, consistent structure, and therapy focusing on emotion regulation can drastically improve outcomes.

Youth with ODD often experience intense frustration, emotional dysregulation, and difficulty managing anger. They may resist authority or seem argumentative, but these behaviors often mask deeper feelings of helplessness or fear. Approaching them with empathy, clear structure, and predictable boundaries can help restore trust and stability.

13. Conduct Disorder

- **Description:** Conduct disorder is a behavioral disorder characterized by persistent patterns of aggression, rule-breaking, deceitfulness, or violation of the rights of others. These behaviors go beyond typical childhood misbehavior and may include physical aggression, destruction of property, lying, or serious disregard for rules and authority.
- **Contribution:** Youth with conduct disorder often experience intense emotional dysregulation, difficulty managing anger, and strained relationships with peers, family, and authority figures. These ongoing conflicts can lead to feelings of isolation, rejection, or hopelessness. When combined with underlying trauma, depression, or substance use, the emotional burden may increase suicide risk.

ODD as intentional defiance rather than emotional struggle can escalate tension and increase mental health risks. Parental empathy, consistent structure, and therapy focusing on emotion regulation can drastically improve outcomes.

It's important to recognize that these behaviors are often expressions of unmet emotional needs rather than intentional defiance. Early intervention, consistent structure, and trauma-informed mental health support can significantly improve outcomes and reduce long-term risk.

14. Autism Spectrum Disorder (ASD)

- **Description:** Autism spectrum disorder is a neurodevelopmental condition that affects communication, social interaction, sensory processing, and behavior. Individuals with ASD may experience differences in how they understand social cues, express emotions, or respond to sensory input. The spectrum is wide, and everyone's experience is unique.
- **Contribution:** Youth with autism spectrum disorder may face increased vulnerability to anxiety, depression, and suicidal ideation—particularly during adolescence—due to social isolation, bullying, or difficulty expressing emotional distress. Challenges with communication can make it harder for them to articulate feelings of sadness or hopelessness, leading emotional pain to go unnoticed.

Providing supportive environments, clear communication, predictable routines, and access to mental health professionals familiar with autism can help reduce distress and foster emotional well-being. Understanding and accommodation—not "fixing"—are key protective factors.

Why Mental Health Conditions Increase Suicide Risk

Mental health conditions often impair cognitive and emotional functioning. They distort perceptions of reality, reduce problem-solving abilities, and amplify emotional pain, leading individuals to believe that suicide is the only way to end their suffering.

While not every young person with a mental health condition experiences suicidal thoughts, certain conditions can increase vulnerability.

Mental health challenges often affect how a person thinks and feels, distorting their sense of reality, limiting problem-solving abilities, and amplifying emotional pain. In those moments, it can feel as though there's no way out, and suicide becomes seen as the only viable option to end the suffering.

Understanding this connection can help caregivers respond with compassion rather than fear. Recognizing that suicidal thoughts often stem from deep emotional pain—not a desire for death itself—allows parents to support their children with empathy and urgency.

Understanding Suicidal Ideation & Prevention

Suicide prevention begins with awareness: learning to recognize early signs of suicidal ideation and understanding how to respond when they appear. This section will guide you through what those warning signs can look like, how to approach the conversation with your child, and what immediate steps you can take to ensure safety and connection.

What is Suicidal Ideation?

"Suicidal ideation" refers to thinking about or formulating plans for suicide. The ideation exists on a spectrum of intensity, beginning with a general desire to die that lacks any concrete method, plan, intention, or action, and progressing to active suicidal ideation, which involves having a detailed plan and a determined intent to act on the ideas laid out within it. Suicidal ideation is closely associated with both suicidal attempts and deaths by suicide, serving as a significant risk factor for future suicide attempts. Suicidal thoughts and actions are often viewed as a single concept; however, passive thinking, active planning, and actual behavior are points along a continuous spectrum.

Research[15] indicates that some individuals attempt suicide without prior suicidal ideation, though this is debatable due to potential underreporting post-attempt for fear of stigmatization. A helpful analogy is to view suicidal ideation as the more significant, yet unseen, portion of an iceberg, with the act of suicide as the visible tip of it. This perspective emphasizes the need for early identification and targeted intervention of those with suicidal ideation to prevent progression to suicide.

Signs of Suicidal Ideation

Suicide prevention begins with awareness: learning to recognize early signs of suicidal ideation and understanding how to respond when they appear. This section will guide you through what those warning signs can look like, how to approach the conversation with your child, and what immediate steps you can take to ensure safety and connection.

[15]Source: https://pubmed.ncbi.nlm.nih.gov/33351435/

What to Look For:

- Sudden increase in reckless behaviors
- Increased alcohol and other substance abuse
- Neglect of self-care or personal hygiene
- Significant changes in eating or sleeping habits
- Isolating from family and friends
- Talking about wanting to die or kill oneself
- Talking about being a burden to others, feeling trapped, or having no reason to live
- Withdrawing from activities they used to enjoy
- Extreme mood swings or irritability
- Slow/quiet speech and movements

Tips for Navigating the Subject Matter

Bringing up the topic of suicide with your child can be daunting, but it's essential to do so with empathy, openness, and honesty. Creating a safe space for conversation where your child feels comfortable expressing their thoughts and feelings without fear of judgment is extremely important. Let them know you're there to listen and support them unconditionally.

Remaining Calm and Composed—Even When You're Not Sure How

When a child expresses emotional pain, distress, or thoughts of suicide, it's completely natural for a parent to feel terrified, panicked, heartbroken, or all the above. We want to lock them in their room and protect them from any harm they may do to themselves. Remaining calm does *not* mean you're not feeling those things. It means you're demonstrating a **grounded self**, acting as a steady, safe presence for your child in that moment.

Here are some ways to stay calm when you may feel anything but:

PAUSE BEFORE REACTING

Take a breath—literally. Inhale slowly through your nose for four seconds, hold your breath in for four seconds, then exhale through your mouth for six to eight seconds. Do this at least three times. This kind of breathwork activates the parasympathetic nervous system, helping your body move out of "fight or flight" mode.

SPEAK MORE SLOWLY THAN YOU NORMALLY WOULD

Your child will be watching you for cues—tone, pacing, and body language. Slowing your speech even just a little communicates that you're present and thinking, not panicking.

NAME YOUR EMOTIONS (PRIVATELY)

Say to yourself, "I am scared right now. This is a lot." Naming what you're feeling—either in your mind or with another trusted adult—helps you move through it with more control.

USE SUPPORTIVE INTERNAL SELF-TALK

You can silently tell yourself:

- *"I can handle this moment."*
- *"My child needs calm, not control."*
- *"It's okay to be scared and steady at the same time."*

These reminders help you self-regulate without denying the real emotions you're feeling.

TOUCH SOMETHING GROUNDING

Hold a cool glass of water, press your feet into the floor, or even hold your child's hand gently. These small sensory acts can help you stay present and focused.

REMIND YOURSELF OF YOUR ROLE

You don't need to have all the answers. Your job in that moment is to *listen, stay with them*, and *keep them safe*. You can figure out next steps together—but only if your child feels secure enough to keep talking.

PRACTICE ACTIVE LISTENING

Give the child your full attention and listen to what they have to say without interrupting or dismissing their feelings (see more detail under Parenting Tools & Strategies, below).

VALIDATE THEIR EMOTIONS

Let the child know it's okay to feel overwhelmed or distressed and that you're there to support them through it. Let them cry. Don't try to "fix it" or shush them.

One of the toughest things to process when our child is hurting is the helplessness we feel when we can't fix them or fix the situation. It's a natural reaction to want to jump in with solutions, reframe their thinking, or offer advice and personal experiences to make it better. We get it. It's hard to read "don't try to fix it" when fixing things is exactly what we want to do. But the best way to actually help is to resist that urge and simply be present. That is the fix.

SET CLEAR BOUNDARIES

While being empathetic and supportive, it's essential to maintain clear boundaries as a parent and avoid being manipulated or coerced into unhealthy behaviors.

This can feel complicated when your child is struggling. The line between genuine distress and behavior designed to avoid consequences isn't always clear — and honestly, it doesn't always have to be. When in doubt, lead with empathy first. But boundaries still matter. A child who learns that expressing distress results in all rules disappearing isn't learning that they're loved, they're learning that distress is a tool. You can hold both things at once: *"I believe you're hurting, and the boundary still stands."*

If you find yourself consistently unsure whether what you're seeing is genuine crisis or manipulation, that's a signal to bring in a professional who can help you read the situation with more clarity and confidence.

SEEK PROFESSIONAL HELP

If you're unsure how to navigate the situation, or if your child's safety is at risk, don't hesitate to seek guidance from mental health professionals who can provide expert support and assistance. A great place to start is with your child's pediatrician or primary care provider. **If your child is in immediate danger, call 911 or take them to the nearest emergency room.**

Navigating the intersection of mental health and suicide prevention as a parent is undoubtedly challenging, but it's also incredibly important. By understanding the signs, fostering open communication, and maintaining clear boundaries, parents can play a vital role in supporting their child's mental well-being and preventing suicide.

Immediate Help (U.S.)

- **Emergency – Call 911** if you or someone you know is in immediate danger.
- **988 Suicide & Crisis Lifeline** — Call or text HOPE to 988 24/7 for yourself or someone you're worried about.

These are the fastest ways to reach help right now.

National Hotlines & Support (U.S.)

- **National Suicide Prevention Lifeline:** 1-800-273-TALK (8255); En español: 1-888-628-9454
- **Crisis Text Line:** Text HELLO to 741741
- **Self-Harm Hotline:** 1-800-DONT-CUT (366-8288)
- **Disaster Distress Helpline:** 1-800-985-5990 (call or text)
- **National Hopeline Network:** 1-800-SUICIDE (784-2433)
- **TREVOR Crisis Line (LGBTQ+ Youth):** 1-866-488-7386
- **National Domestic Violence Hotline:** 1-800-799-7233
- **National Crisis Line – Anorexia & Bulimia:** 1-800-233-4357
- **National Council on Alcoholism & Drug Dependency Hopeline:** 1-800-622-2255 (call or text)
- **Veterans Crisis Line:** Call 1-800-273-TALK (8255) and press 1, or text **838255**

glow for HOPE

For more resources visit GlowForHopeNFP.org

PART III: PARENTING TOOLS & STRATEGIES

How to Talk to Your Child About Hard Topics

Talking about mental health—especially when your child might be struggling—can feel intimidating, even for the most loving parent. You may worry about saying the wrong thing, making things worse, or not knowing how to respond if your child opens up about something painful. But the truth is, starting the conversation is often the single most important step you can take.

These discussions aren't about having all the answers. They're about creating safety, showing empathy, and letting your child know you're ready to listen without judgment. One of the most powerful ways to do that is by practicing **active listening**.

Active Listening: Building Stronger Connections

When conversations turn serious, how we listen matters just as much as what we say. Active listening is the process of fully concentrating on, understanding, responding to, and remembering what's being said. Active listening shows your child that their voice and feelings truly matter.

What Is Active Listening?

Active listening means being present in the moment and giving your child your full attention. That means avoiding distractions (like your phone), and maintaining eye contact, using body language that says, "I'm here, and I care." When we listen this way, we make space for honesty and emotional safety, which foster trust.

The Key Components of Active Listening

1. PAY ATTENTION.

Give your child your undivided attention. Turn toward them, make eye contact, and avoid multitasking. When they see you're 100% focused on them, they will know that what they're saying is important.

2. SHOW YOU'RE LISTENING.

Nonverbal cues matter. Nodding occasionally, maintaining an open posture, and keeping a gentle facial expression can reassure them that you're engaged and not judging.

3. PROVIDE FEEDBACK.

Reflect back what you're hearing to make sure you understand correctly. You might say, "It sounds like you're feeling left out," or "What I'm hearing is that school has been really stressful lately." This helps clarify feelings and prevents misunderstandings.

4. DEFER JUDGMENT.

Let your child finish their thoughts before you respond. Avoid interrupting, correcting, or offering solutions. Silence can sometimes feel uncomfortable, but giving loved ones time and room to talk can encourage them to share more openly.

5. RESPOND APPROPRIATELY.

When you do speak, keep your tone calm and caring. Be honest, but gentle. You can share your perspective without minimizing theirs. For example, you might say: "I can see why you'd feel that way. Let's figure out what could help."

Why Active Listening Matters

When parents practice active listening, it builds trust, strengthens relationships, and helps children feel seen and understood. It also reduces conflict and prevents escalation by keeping the focus on connection rather than correction. Listening in this way models empathy, which is one of the most powerful tools for emotional resilience.

Practical Tips for Everyday Conversations

- Maintain eye contact and put away distractions. That means putting your phone down, turning the TV off, not glancing back and forth at your computer. It means 100% attention to the conversation. Be present.
- Be patient; pauses often mean your child is deciding whether it's safe to share more.
- Ask open-ended questions that invite dialogue, such as "What's been the hardest part of your week?" or "Can you tell me more about that?"
- Avoid judgmental phrases like "You're overreacting" or "You shouldn't feel that way."

Examples of Conversation Starters

- "I've noticed you've seemed really down lately, and I'm worried about you. Can we talk about what's been going on?"
- "You've been on my mind a lot recently. How are you really doing? I'm here to listen if you want to talk."
- "It seems like you're carrying a lot right now. Is there anything you'd like to share? I want to make sure you're okay because I care about you."
- "I've been reading about how important it is to talk about mental health. How have you been feeling lately?"
- "You matter to me. Have you had any thoughts about hurting yourself or feeling hopeless?"

Validating Emotions Without Overpromising

After your child begins to open up, your next step is to help them feel truly heard. Validation means acknowledging what your child is feeling, even if you don't fully understand or agree with it. When you validate their emotions, you're saying, "I see you. I believe that your feelings are real, and they matter."

Validation isn't about fixing the problem or instantly making things better; it's about letting your child know they're not alone in what they feel. It bridges the gap between your experience and theirs, especially during moments of distress or misunderstanding.

What Validation Sounds Like

- "That sounds really hard. I can understand why you'd feel upset."
- "It makes sense that you're frustrated. Anyone would feel that way in your situation."
- "I can tell this means a lot to you."
- "Thank you for telling me. That must have taken courage."

These kinds of statements show empathy without trying to solve the problem right away. Sometimes, what your child needs most is your presence, not your advice.

Avoiding Common Pitfalls

Parents often invalidate feelings without realizing it. Phrases like "It's not that bad," "You're overreacting," or "You'll get over it" can unintentionally shut your child down. Even well-meaning reassurances like "Everything will be fine" can feel dismissive when your child is in pain.

Instead, try responses that keep the door open:

- "I'm really sorry this is happening. Let's work through it together."
- "I may not know exactly how you feel, but I want to understand."
- "You don't have to go through this alone."

Validation helps your child feel emotionally safe—a critical foundation for healing and resilience.

Balancing Empathy and Realism

While validation acknowledges your child's feelings, overpromising can lead to mistrust. Avoid guarantees like "I promise this will never happen again" or "I'll make sure everything's okay." Instead, focus on what you *can* promise: your love, your support, and your effort to help them find the right tools and resources.

FOR EXAMPLE: "I can't fix this overnight, but I'll be here every step of the way, and we'll figure out what can help."

Why Validation Matters

When children feel heard and understood, their emotional intensity naturally decreases. They begin to believe their feelings are manageable rather than overwhelming. This is how emotional regulation develops: not through suppression, but through acknowledgment.

Validation also strengthens your personal relationship, making it more likely that your child will turn to you again in the future. Over time, this consistent practice will become one of your most powerful tools for building connection and trust.

Teaching Problem-Solving & Building Resilience

- **Identify the Problem:**

  EXAMPLE: "I see that you're having trouble with your homework. Let's figure out what specifically is causing the difficulty."

  HOW TO DO IT:
  Ask Questions: Encourage your child to articulate the problem by asking questions like, "What exactly is bothering you?" or "Can you tell me more about what happened?"

  Break It Down: Help them break the problem into smaller, more manageable parts.

- **Brainstorm Solutions:**

  EXAMPLE: "What are some ways we could solve this problem? Let's list all the ideas that come to mind, even the ones that seem silly."

  HOW TO DO IT:
  Encourage Creativity: Encourage your child to think of as many solutions as possible without judging or dismissing any ideas initially.

  Write It Down: Write down all of the potential solutions to help to visually organize their thoughts.

- **Evaluate the Solutions:**

  EXAMPLE: "Let's go through each of these ideas and think about the pros and cons. Which ones do you think might work best?"

  HOW TO DO IT:
  Discuss Consequences: Discuss the potential outcomes of each solution. Ask questions like, "What do you think will happen if we try this?" or "Are there any downsides to this idea?"

  Weigh Options: Help them weigh the pros and cons of each solution.

- **Choose a Solution:**
  EXAMPLE: "Based on our discussion, which solution do you want to try first?"

  HOW TO DO IT:
  Empower Decision-Making: Encourage your child to choose a solution based on the evaluation.

  Support Their Choice: Respect their decision and support them in trying it out.

- **Implement the Solution:**
  EXAMPLE: "Now that we've chosen a solution, what steps do we need to take to put it into action?"

HOW TO DO IT:

Plan Steps: Help your child plan the specific steps needed to implement the chosen solution.

Take Action Together: If appropriate, work together to carry out the plan.

- **Evaluate the Outcome:**

EXAMPLE: "Let's see how well our solution worked. What went well and what could have been better?"

HOW TO DO IT:

Reflect: Encourage your child to reflect on the outcome of their decision.

Discuss Adjustments: Talk about what could be adjusted or tried differently next time.

- **Encourage Persistence and Flexibility:**

EXAMPLE: "Sometimes our first idea doesn't work out. That's okay. What else can we try?"

HOW TO DO IT:

Normalize Setbacks: Teach your child that setbacks are a normal part of problem-solving.

Encourage Adaptability: Encourage them to be flexible and try new solutions if the first one doesn't work.

Combining Guidance with Independence

While guiding your child through this process, it's essential to balance providing help with fostering independence. Gradually give them more responsibility for each step as they become more confident in their problem-solving abilities. This approach not only teaches them how to handle challenges effectively but also builds their confidence and resilience.

Supporting Unique Needs

Every child will experience the world in their own way. Their personalities, cultures, identities, and lived experiences shape how they understand and express emotions. For some children, these differences can also influence how they experience mental health challenges and how comfortable they feel asking for help.

As caregivers, our role is to recognize and honor those unique experiences. That means learning to see through multiple lenses—culture, gender identity, neurodiversity, family structure, faith, and more—so we can respond with both compassion and understanding.

Supporting a child's mental health isn't a one-size-fits-all process. The strategies that help one child thrive might not work for another, and that's okay. What matters most is showing your child that who they are is seen, accepted, and valued. When they know their full identity is respected, they will be far more likely to trust you, open up to you, and believe they deserve support.

Creating Safe and Affirming Spaces

A supportive home is the foundation of a child's mental well-being. Acceptance and affirmation go beyond love; they communicate safety. For LGBTQ+ youth, this may mean using their preferred names and pronouns. For BIPOC youth, it can mean celebrating cultural heritage and affirming racial identity.

When parents create an environment where children can express who they are without fear of judgment or rejection, this environment becomes a powerful protective factor against depression, anxiety, and self-harm.

Understanding the Impact of Discrimination

Bullying, harassment, or discrimination, whether based on race, ethnicity, gender identity, or sexual orientation, can have lasting effects on mental health. For LGBTQ+ and BIPOC teens, systemic inequities often compound daily stresses and isolation.

Parents and caregivers can't erase those systems, but they can advocate within schools, faith communities, and peer networks to make sure their children are treated with dignity. Simply saying, "What happened to you is not okay, and it's not your fault," helps restore a sense of safety and worth to the child.

Seeking Culturally Responsive Mental Health Care

When looking for professional help, cultural understanding matters. BIPOC youth benefit from therapists who are aware of racial trauma, family dynamics, and community pressures. LGBTQ+ youth may need providers who affirm identity and understand coming-out stress as well as gender dysphoria.

When calling for appointments, parents can ask:

- "Do your counselors have experience working with LGBTQ+ teens?"
- "Does your practice address racial or cultural identity as part of treatment?"

These simple questions help ensure your child receives care that honors their full self.

The Power of Family Acceptance

Family acceptance is one of the strongest protective factors for youth mental health. Research shows that LGBTQ+ teens who feel accepted by their families are significantly less likely to experience suicidal thoughts or attempts. The overall principle extends to all families—unconditional love, patient listening, and reassurance that your child is worthy, *exactly as they are*, can be life-saving.

If your teen senses that home is a safe place to talk about identity, they are more likely to reach out before a crisis.

Breaking the Stigma in BIPOC Communities

In some cultures, mental health is still a taboo topic. Seeking help may be seen as a weakness or "airing family business." These beliefs can prevent youth from speaking up until problems escalate. Parents can challenge stigma by normalizing conversations about emotions, therapy, and stress management.

Sharing your own experiences with anxiety or sadness—or simply expressing, "Everyone struggles sometimes, and getting help is brave"—teaches that mental health is a component of overall health.

Understanding Intersectionality

Many teens hold multiple marginalized identities—for instance, being both LGBTQ+ and BIPOC—and face overlapping stressors such as racism, homophobia, or transphobia.

These compounded pressures can increase vulnerability to anxiety, depression, or suicidal thoughts. Recognizing intersectionality helps parents approach each situation with humility and empathy. You don't need to have all the answers; what matters is listening and validating the complexity of your child's experience.

Community Support as a Protective Factor

Resilience often grows in community. Connection with peers who "get it" reminds youth that they are not alone. Encourage participation in cultural clubs, LGBTQ+ youth centers, or affirming faith-based groups. These spaces can reinforce pride, belonging, and hope—powerful counterbalances to isolation.

Recognizing Heightened Suicide Risk

Because of ongoing discrimination and social rejection, LGBTQ+ and BIPOC youth experience disproportionately high rates of suicidal ideation and attempts. Pay close attention to signs of withdrawal, hopelessness, or talk of being a burden.

If you notice warning signs, seek professional help immediately, preferably from providers experienced in these communities. Early, culturally competent intervention saves lives.

Key Takeaway

Every child's story is unique. By offering empathy, curiosity, and affirmation—especially in moments when the world may not—you teach your child that their identity is not a problem to solve but a truth to be honored. Your consistent support becomes the thread of hope that can carry them through even the hardest days.

Navigating Risky Behaviors

Adolescence is a time of exploration, and sometimes that exploration can lead to choices that put a young person's safety or well-being at risk. Behaviors like experimenting with drugs or alcohol, self-harm, unsafe sexual activity, or online engagement with harmful content often stem from deeper emotional pain rather than simple rebellion.

When we recognize these behaviors as signals rather than defiance, we can respond with curiosity and care instead of punishment. Asking "What might my child be trying to cope with?" opens a door to understanding the root of the behavior, which is the first step toward healing.

Substance Use and Self-Medication

Many teens turn to alcohol, vaping, or drugs not to "act out," but to numb anxiety, trauma, or depression. These substances may temporarily dull the pain, but they will also deepen feelings of hopelessness and isolation over time.

INSTEAD OF JUMPING STRAIGHT TO DISCIPLINE, BEGIN WITH EMPATHY AND OBSERVATION:

"I've noticed you've been drinking more lately. I'm not angry—I'm concerned. What's been going on?"

Offer help without shame, and when needed, reach out to healthcare providers or counselors who specialize in adolescent substance use. Early intervention can prevent lifelong patterns.

Self-Harm

Self-harm, such as cutting, burning, or hitting oneself, is often a way to release emotional pain or regain a sense of control. While it can be frightening to discover, responding with anger or fear may push your child further away.

FOCUS INSTEAD ON SAFETY AND UNDERSTANDING:

"I can see you're hurting, and I'm here to help you find a safer way to cope."

It is recommended to remove tools they might use for self-harm, while at the same time replacing them with coping alternatives: stress balls, grounding exercises, journaling, or talking with a therapist. Remember: self-harm is not about seeking attention, it's a sign of deep distress that needs compassion and professional care.

Online and Social Media Risks

Today's youth live much of their emotional lives online. Social media can connect and inspire them, but it can also expose them to bullying, unrealistic comparisons, or predatory behaviors.

TALK WITH YOUR CHILD ABOUT HOW CERTAIN CONTENT MAKES THEM FEEL. ASK:

"When you're scrolling through TikTok or Instagram, do you feel better or worse afterward?"

Encourage regular "digital detox" moments and establish clear, respectful boundaries around devices. Emphasize that moderation and safety online are acts of self-care, not control.

Peer Pressure and Identity Experimentation

Adolescence is also about belonging. Sometimes risky choices have to do with fitting in or finding identity. If your child starts hanging out with a new crowd, changing how they dress, or pushing limits, resist the urge to react defensively. Instead, get curious:

"I see you've been spending more time with new friends. What do you like about them?"

Curiosity communicates respect and invites honesty. You may discover that what looks like rebellion is actually a search for connection.

Balancing Boundaries with Empathy

Teens need structure just as much as they need understanding. Boundaries create safety, but they work best when enforced with empathy. Let your child know why the boundary exists:

"I know you want independence. My job is to keep you safe while you learn how to handle that freedom."

Use consistent consequences without humiliation, and always pair discipline with reassurance of love and belief in their ability to grow.

When to Seek Professional Help

If risky behaviors become patterns, or you sense your child is in danger, it's time to seek help. Look for therapists who specialize in adolescent behavior and trauma-informed care. Involve your child in the process of choosing a counselor whenever possible; it builds trust and increases the likelihood of participation.

For immediate safety concerns, call 911 or go to your nearest emergency department. You don't have to handle it alone.

Risky behaviors may be your child's current way of saying, "Something hurts." Responding with empathy, consistency, and professional support teaches them that their mistakes do not define them. Instead, they learn that even in their darkest moments, they are still worthy of love, safety, and a path forward.

Partnering with Schools & Professionals

No parent should have to navigate their child's mental health journey alone. Schools, counselors, and healthcare professionals can be powerful allies. But families often need guidance on how to access the right help and build effective partnerships. Knowing where to start and how to advocate well will make a world of difference in your child's care and confidence.

Collaborating With Schools

Teachers, school counselors, and administrators are often among the first to notice when a student is struggling. Regular communication between parents and school staff helps ensure that emotional and academic needs are addressed early.

If your child has ongoing challenges with focus, anxiety, or emotional regulation, consider requesting a meeting to discuss possible supports, such as a 504 Plan or Individualized Education Program (IEP). These formal plans can provide classroom accommodations, like flexible deadlines, access to quiet spaces, or regular counseling check-ins.

When meeting with teachers or staff, try framing conversations as teamwork:

"Here's what we're noticing at home. What have you observed in class? How can we work together to support them?"

This collaborative approach keeps everyone focused on solutions rather than blame, and it ensures your child feels supported from every angle.

When to Seek Professional Help

Sometimes, the challenges your child faces go beyond what family and schools can manage alone. If emotional outbursts, withdrawal, or risky behaviors persist despite your efforts, it may be time to involve a mental health professional.

Look for licensed clinicians experienced in working with adolescents and families. Ask about their approach and whether they specialize in areas relevant to your child's needs (such as anxiety, depression, trauma, or identity development). You might start with your pediatrician, who can refer you to trusted mental health providers.

glow FOR HOPE *Visit the Glow For Hope Resource Hub for more support.*

It can help to tell your child,

"We're bringing in someone who knows more about these things than we do, just like we'd see a doctor if you broke your arm."

This normalizes therapy and positions it as an act of care, not punishment.

Creating and Using a Family Crisis Plan

Even in the most supportive homes, moments of crisis can arise. A family safety plan — sometimes called a crisis plan — ensures everyone knows what to do if your child becomes unsafe or experiences suicidal thoughts. Having one in place before a moment of crisis hits means you're not trying to figure it out in the middle of one.

To help families do exactly that, we have developed the **Glow For Hope Safety Support Plan** — a family-centered tool that walks you through each element of a solid safety plan in one easy-to-use document.

Your plan should include:

- **Warning signs** that a crisis might be developing (e.g., social withdrawal, hopeless talk, sudden calmness after distress).
- **Coping strategies** your child finds helpful (breathing exercises, music, grounding activities).
- **Emergency contacts,** including trusted adults, therapist, pediatrician, and local crisis lines.
- **Crisis resources** such as 988 (Suicide & Crisis Lifeline) and the nearest hospital or mental health center.

The Glow For Hope Safety Support Plan is designed to help you identify each of these and organize emergency steps — all in one place. Keep a copy somewhere visible and easy to reach, reviewing it together regularly.

Remind your child that a crisis plan isn't about expecting the worst — it's about being prepared and staying safe, just like practicing a fire drill.

Download the Glow For Hope Safety Support Plan at GlowForHopeNFP.org

Advocating for Your Child's Needs

Advocacy is about persistence and partnership. Don't hesitate to ask questions, request clarity, or seek second opinions. You know your child best.

When navigating appointments or school meetings, consider keeping a simple notebook or digital log of conversations, recommendations, and follow-ups. It helps you stay organized and ensures that nothing falls through the cracks.

If you ever feel dismissed or unheard, you have every right to request another provider or to escalate your concerns. Advocacy is commitment. It says, "My child's well-being matters too much to let this go."

When families, schools, and professionals work together, children gain a safety net of understanding and support. By building consistent communication and proactive plans, you're showing your child that mental health is a community effort, an effort rooted in love, teamwork, and hope.

Part V: Support for Parents

Parenting through mental health challenges can feel overwhelming. It's natural to focus all your energy on your child's needs, but without caring for yourself as well, burnout and hopelessness can easily set in.

Remember, you cannot pour from an empty cup. Your well-being directly affects your child's ability to heal, grow, and trust that stability in life is possible.

Caring for Yourself

Caring for a struggling child can bring waves of fear, guilt, frustration, and exhaustion. Many parents wonder if they're doing enough and if they're doing it right. You're doing something extraordinary simply by showing up, again and again, for someone who needs you.

Self-care for parents is a means of survival. It's how you will maintain the strength to keep supporting your child over the long term. That care doesn't have to be dramatic. Small, intentional acts can make a real difference.

Try starting with these:

- **Set realistic expectations.** You can't fix everything, and that's okay. Focus on progress, not perfection.
- **Take short breaks.** Step outside, stretch, or breathe deeply for a few minutes. Rest isn't a reward; it's a requirement.
- **Stay connected.** Isolation fuels shame. Reach out to a trusted friend, faith leader, or counselor for honest conversation.
- **Acknowledge your emotions**. It's okay to feel angry, scared, or sad. Allow yourself to process those feelings instead of pushing them away.

If you notice persistent signs of anxiety, depression, or hopelessness in yourself, please seek professional support. Many parents find therapy invaluable for processing their own fears and learning new coping tools. Caring for your own mental health is part of caring for your family's.

Remember:

You don't have to be a perfect parent. You only need to be a present one.

Building a Support Network

It takes courage to admit you need help, but no parent should have to do this alone. A strong support network is one of the greatest and most bountiful protective factors for both you and your child.

Your network can include:

- **Family and Friends:** Share openly about what's happening. People often want to help but don't know how. Give them specific ways to show up for you.
- **Other Parents:** Connecting with others who've faced similar challenges can be incredibly validating. Support groups, whether in-person or online, remind you that you're not the only one walking this road.
- **Faith or Community Leaders:** If faith is part of your life, lean into those relationships for encouragement and prayer, as long as the environment feels safe and nonjudgmental.
- **Professionals:** Therapists, case managers, and school counselors can guide you through systems that often feel confusing or intimidating.

When you build a network of support, you create a circle of stability that benefits both you and your child.

You might say to someone you trust:

"I'm doing my best, but I could use someone to check in with once a week. Would you be okay with that?"

That one regular conversation can become a lifeline.

Finding Strength in Shared Hope

Healing rarely happens in isolation. As you learn to prioritize your own care and to surround yourself with support, you model resilience for your child within your family setting and demonstrate the gifts of being active in your community. You show them that strength doesn't mean doing everything alone, it means knowing when to reach out and letting others help you carry the weight.

Your courage will be called upon to keep showing up for your child and for yourself. Each act of courage can plant a seed of hope that will grow in both of you.

PART VI: MOVING FORWARD IN HOPE

Embracing Hope and Healing Together

It's important to remember that navigating your child's mental health journey is a path paved with challenges, learning, and profound love. The steps you take today, no matter how small they may seem, are significant strides toward healing, understanding, and resilience for both you and your child.

Embracing the Journey

Remember, this journey is not one you embark upon alone. Along the way, you'll encounter allies—healthcare providers, teachers, family members, and organizations like **Glow For Hope**—who are here to walk beside you.

Glow For Hope creates safe, welcoming spaces through events that foster connection, conversation, and community. These moments of coming together remind us that healing happens not only in clinical settings, but also in the everyday acts of showing up, supporting one another, and sharing lived experiences.

When the path feels overwhelming, these connections can serve as your anchors—reminders that hope, understanding, and support are within reach.

Community engagement helps reduce stigma and increases access to resources, which can be particularly beneficial for families navigating mental health challenges.[16]

[16]Corrigan et al., 2014

Cultivating Resilience and Hope

Resilience is not an innate trait, but a quality forged through adversity, learning, and growth. By adopting the strategies outlined in this guide, you're not only helping your child to navigate their current struggles but also instilling in them the resilience they need for the future. Each day brings new opportunities for growth, healing, and joy.

Embrace these moments, celebrate small victories, and remain hopeful about the future.

Hope is a psychological resource that has been shown to enhance well-being and resilience. Research on hope distinguishes between two essential components: **agency**—the belief that you have the will to move toward a goal—and **pathways**—the ability to find routes to get there.[17] As a parent, you can nurture both in your child. When you say, "I know this is hard, and I believe you can find a way through it," you are actively teaching your child how to hope. Hope is not passive. It is something you practice together, in small moments of encouragement, in the willingness to try again after a setback, and in the daily act of showing up.

The Power of Love and Understanding

Above all, your love, understanding, and unwavering support are the most powerful gifts you can offer your child. Your presence, empathy, and compassion remind them they are not defined by their mental health challenges; rather, they are cherished for who they are.

Perhaps most encouraging is that a parent's hopeful outlook is genuinely contagious. Children who witness their caregivers approaching difficulty with steady optimism are more likely to internalize that same orientation

[17] Snyder et al., 2002

over time—even when they cannot yet feel it themselves. You don't need to pretend everything is fine. What matters is modeling the belief that things can get better, and that the path forward, even if not yet visible, exists.

This unconditional love is the foundation upon which they can build their recovery and envision a future filled with possibilities.

A Continuous Journey of Learning and Support

The journey of parenting a child with mental health challenges is one of continuous learning and adaptation. Stay informed, seek out new resources, and be open to evolving your strategies as you gain more insights into your child's needs.

Remember, it's okay to seek help for yourself too. Caring for your well-being is essential to being there effectively for your child, and the caregiver's mental health is equally important. Research shows that caregivers of children with mental health issues are at higher risk of experiencing stress, anxiety, and depression themselves. The acts of seeking support and practicing self-care are essential for maintaining their well-being and their ability to care for their child.[18]

Remember to visit the Glow For Hope Resource Hub often as we will be continually adding resources.

[18]Raina et al., 2005

Looking Forward & With Gratitude

As we close this guide, we do so with full hearts — grateful for the many hands that shaped these pages, and hopeful for every family who will hold them.

This guide would not exist without the generosity of many. We are grateful to the clinicians, parents, caregivers, advocates, and survivors who offered their expertise, their lived experience, and their time. To our board, our volunteers, and our community partners — thank you for believing in this work. And, to the St. Clair County Mental Health Board, whose support made this resource possible — we are deeply grateful.

The road ahead for your family may be uncertain, but it is also filled with potential for healing and happiness. Together, with patience, understanding, and love, you and your child can navigate the complexities of mental health and move toward a brighter, hopeful horizon.

To every parent, grandparent, guardian, and caregiver who has ever sat up at 3 a.m. wondering if they're doing enough — the fact that you're still asking that question means you're exactly who this child needs.

Glow For Hope NFP
GlowForHopeNFP.org | @glowforhope

www.ingramcontent.com/pod-product-compliance
Lightning Source LLC
LaVergne TN
LVHW050939210926
848482LV00013B/676
* 9 7 8 0 9 9 6 7 2 0 2 3 6 *